LIGHTNING

STRUCK TWICE

LIGHTNING STRUCK TWICE

First Edition

Shawntae Sawyer

Revival Waves of Glory Books & Publishing
PO Box 596
Litchfield, IL 62056
United States of America
www.revivalwavesofgloryministries.com

Revival Waves of Glory Books & Publishing is committed to excellence in the publishing industry.

Published in the United States of America

Paperback: 978-1-365-82792-1

Table of Contents

DEDICATIONS
ACKNOWLEDGEMENTS

Thank GOD for giving me the strength to write this book and tell my story. I cried many days and nights trying to complete this book. I dedicate this book to Neichelle and Malikah. No child should be told to keep a secret when they are physically, emotionally, verbally, and or sexually abused. It is never ok for someone to abuse or misuse you. Donald (my dad) sorry you missed seeing me grow up and develop into this beautiful woman, Lavonda, Ms Johnnie, Almatina, and Leslie, thank you for being true friends. John and Kathy who's always willing to make time to listen and give me advice. My ex-husband I apologize for the hurt I caused due to being misled. Tramel E, Thank you for all the days and nights you motivated me to finish this book, for the sunshine you brought into my life and always willing to shield me from the rain during our rainy days.

For the loved ones who ran their race and has come to an end: My aunt Patricia, My grandfather Joe, My uncle Timmy, and My uncle David- REST IN PEACE.

For comments about the book or if you want to get your ton of bricks off your chest I would love to hear from you:

nomoabuse2014@gmail.com

Chapter One

My name is Shawny, born August 4, 1978, to the parents of Renee and Ducky at ages seventeen. At age two, Renee and Ducky decided to part ways. Renee met a man named Keith, that she soon would begin dating. Keith was a man who would have been any woman's dream man. He was twenty-eight years old, gainfully employed, a homeowner, drove a nice vehicle, wore a uniform to work, and had no kids. My mom was nineteen years old, a single mother, with a recent failed relationship with the father of her child; she thought she had found the man of her dreams. She didn't hesitate to move from her mother's house into Keith's house. She packed her belongings and mine too.

Three years later, my mom had a baby girl by Keith. She seemed to be so happy with Keith; I didn't know my mother's happiness would cost me my childhood. I wasn't really allowed to play with my new baby sister. Keith had said, "I might get jealous and hurt her." By age seven, Keith became very abusive. He abused me, mentally, physically, emotionally, verbally and sexually. That man that was once nice turned into a monster. He decided it was best I didn't see Ducky, my biological father anymore, my mom agreed. At this time, Keith started doing things that a man shouldn't do to a child. I would find myself alone with him; he would send my mom out the house and send my little sister out the room so he and I could be alone. I would tell my sister, "next time he tells you to leave the room, don't leave."

There were a few times my little sister would remember me telling her not to leave so she would say no when he would tell her to leave the room. During these times when she wouldn't leave the room, he would grab a pillow or sheet, put it across his lap and have me sit next to him while my hand would be in his pants. Keith would tell me to open my mouth while he put his mouth to mine, put his tongue in my mouth and start moving his head from side to side, while that was going on he would unzip his pants and pull out what I later learned was a penis and put my hand on it and force my hand to go up and down on it. I didn't know what I was doing. Keith told me, "that's how you French kiss and this is how you make a man feel good." During these acts, Keith would always tell me, "don't tell your mother; because you don't want to hurt her, do you?" I would say, "No."

These physical encounters happened several times... not just in his house, in the vehicle also. He got so bold with his actions that he would come into my room, wake me up to bring me in the bedroom that he and my mom shared together. It would be dark in the room; he laid on the bed and told me to lay next to him. He would start French kissing me, put my hand on his penis, and tell me to move it up and down. I would start saying my hand is getting tired so he would tell me to use the other hand. He would rush me back to my room, saying, "Hurry up, your mom is on her way back, go back in your room and pretend you were sleep."

I was so confused because whenever my mom was around he treated me like the worst child that ever was born. He would constantly yell at me, put a belt or extension cord to my backside, and made me stand in the corner for hours at a time, sometimes even standing on one leg. He would put a belt or extension cord to my backside for any reason such as losing a hat/glove, not eating all my food, missing a spot when cleaning, and not coming fast enough when he would call me. I would be sitting on the toilet and if he called me, I had to stop what I was doing to come see what he wanted. Most of the time he would call me to get him a beer out the fridge or ice out of the freezer. My mom never questioned the way he discipline me. She joined in and used the belt and extension cord to parts of my body. While she would be using the belt or extension cord, I would cry on the inside and outside, thinking to myself, if she only knew how much I love her.

I loved her enough not to tell her what Keith was doing to me when she was not around. I knew parts of his body that a child should not have known but I continued to keep it inside.

Chapter Two

Two years had went by with the same sexual acts going on along with the physical and emotional abuse. One day my mom, Keith and I, went to his job to help him clean up an office building. He had the key to get in. While at his job, my mom looked at me and said, "who is doing something to you." I looked at her and said, "no body." She asked me again I said, "nobody" again, she grabbed me in my collar, looked me in my eyes and asked me a third time, by this time Keith had walked up, heard her ask me and saw her holding me in my collar, he said, "you better tell her". Me being nine years old constantly being abused, the same man who would put a belt or extension cord to my backside, had me stand in the corner for hours at a time, would tell me not to tell my mom, so I wouldn't hurt her, while he's enjoying the pleasure of me, a child playing with his penis and French kissing me as he called it when she wasn't around. So after he told me "you better tell it," I immediately said, "He did and pointed to him." He then denied it and said, "No, I didn't she is lying." My mom grabbed a broom and started hitting him with it. While she was hitting him with the broom, she would say, "why?" Why would you do this to me? I started crying, while feeling relieved. I hated to keep that from my mom. It felt like a ton of bricks was lifted off my chest. Keith was right, I did hurt my mother. He was arrested. He did finally admit the things I said were true. My mom felt so sorry for him she paid the bond to get him out, wrote a letter to the judge saying, "he apologized; we are going to be a family and we would go to counseling." He got off with probation. He stated the reason for the abuse he did to me is due to the alcohol and drugs he was using. Yes, he admitted to being an alcoholic and drug user. I later found out he introduced my mother to be a drugs user. Almost a year later after telling my mom what Keith had done to me, they decided to get married. My sister and I were the flower girls in the wedding. He stopped going to see his counselor, while I continued, not understanding why he stopped and I continued. He did apologize to me and asked me to forgive him, he stated the drugs and alcohol is the reason for the things he did to me, he then asked if he could adopt me. My mom sitting there with us, giving him permission to adopt me. I said, "no I know who my father is." I didn't see my father that much growing up, but I knew when I did see him he never touched me in an inappropriate way, never made me stand in a corner, never raised his voice at me, and never put a belt or extension cord to my backside. My mom forgave him so what was I to do. I forgave him also. I still gave him the up most respect, called him my stepfather.

CHAPTER THREE

So growing up I was taught how to hide the abuse, keep it inside of me and go on like nothing ever happened. I was told not to talk about it. Things did get better. Keith would just ignore me when I did something he didn't like. No more corners, no more belts or extension cords (unless it was from my mom), best of all, no more hands in the pants, or French kissing. We started going to Church. We went to Sunday service, Bible study, and choir rehearsal. We would even study the Bible as a family at home. The first scripture I was taught and memorized was Psalm 23. They even decided we would get baptized as a family. So here, it is I'm Twelve years old, not understanding baptism. I said, "do I have to, I don't want to get baptized," I was told I'm getting baptized and that was the end of the discussion. So I got baptized.

During this time, we had no idea what was coming next. My mom had an affair, during that affair she conceived twins. She told Keith what she had done, they decided to stay married and Keith would raise the twins as his own. The twins were born identical. Again, Keith made the decision that the twins shouldn't be in their biological father's life, Renee (my mom) agreed. So Keith raised them as his own, giving them his last name and they called him dad. Two years went past I got my first job as a server. I continued to work throughout high school, finally graduated from high school. I moved out, got my first apartment.

CHAPTER FOUR

Not long after I met this man whom I began dating. He moved in very quickly. We went to the courthouse got married (April 1st, 1998). After getting married we went home, I called my mother and told her I was married, she said, "ha ha April fool's, I said its no April fool's." I said, "I'm married for real." She said, "I wanted to be there to experience that with you." I said, "well we are going to have a gathering so we can invite people." She was so disappointed and she got off the phone with me. She later got over it (so I thought). We had our first child who turned out to be a baby girl. My mother and I discussed her babysitting our baby, her grandchild while my husband and I went to work. We agreed to pay her $100 per week. She started watching our daughter after being just three weeks old. My husband asked me to stay at home and raise our daughter; I explained two incomes are better than one. He was a little skeptical at first because of what Keith had done to me as a child. I explained to my husband, Keith said he did those things to me because of the alcohol and drugs he was using at the time and he no longer do those things, besides after he apologized he said he would never do that again and he didn't. I mentioned to my mom the doubts my husband was having about her babysitting our daughter in her home with her husband, my mother told me she wouldn't allow her husband to be alone with her, under no circumstance. She said, "I wouldn't allow anything to happen to my grandchild." I had told my husband what my mom said, he said to me with a very serious look, "I don't know what I would do if what happened to you would happen to our daughter." We allowed my mom to babysit our daughter for six months. Due to my mom, beginning to use drugs, some mornings when I would show up to drop my daughter off my mom wouldn't be there and her husband or my brothers constantly turned me away. So my husband and I decided to find another babysitter. My husband knew a woman who had look after his niece. I called her; she didn't hesitate to accept my daughter into her home. She said $60 per week would be fine. Unfortunately my mom wasn't happy with the decision that we had made, so out of spite she called the child protective service to report my husband was molesting our daughter and we were allowing our daughter to be watched by a woman who let dogs urinate, and have bowel movements all over the house while her granddaughter would crawl around in it. We spoke with the social worker who had to do an investigation; she also went to the babysitter's home to look around. Her investigation was completed, no wrongdoing was found, but it has to stay on file. I was very upset with my mom. I stayed away and didn't talk to her for a while. We finally started back talking never mentioned the investigation. When my husband and I would take our daughter to visit my mom, my husband would have to sit in the car in their driveway, he wasn't allowed to step foot in their house. One day Keith, my mom husband, came to me and said, "we don't want him in our driveway anymore he need to wait for you up the street." I couldn't understand why they would decide something like that. My husband didn't understand either.

CHAPTER FIVE

Three years later we had another daughter. My mom was upset with us having another baby, asking me why would I have another baby by him. Keith and my mom would tell me how my husband didn't love me, and how he would have other women in our home while I was at work. My husband and I never discussed cheating, another woman or another man we never questioned. But listening to the people that raised me, listening to the mother who claimed she loved me and didn't protect me as a child suddenly wants to protect me now. She would tell me, he isn't the man for me, and I need to get away from him. I heard it so much; I decided to date a low life outside of my husband. I later told my husband. He said, "we can work it out." I decided I wanted to end our marriage. Deep down inside, I didn't want to leave my husband, the little bit I knew about love I wanted to share it with him.

I constantly would hear my mom say to Keith "you molested my daughter." I would hear Keith say, "Renee you had an affair and had twin boys by another man." I knew this wasn't the marriage I wanted to have, constantly being reminded of my wrongdoing. My mom went with me to my lawyer's office, helped me pay for the lawyer, and even went to my court dates with me. A year later when I got the letter in the mail stating I was divorced, I immediately called my mom and said, "mom, I'm divorced I got the letter in the mail." My mom said, "honey you was a fool, you had you a good husband, ain't no way I would have left my husband," and hung up the phone. I sat there holding the phone thinking about all the things my mom had said about him while we were married. That was the first time I heard my mom say something good about my now ex-husband. As time went on, I remembered that's my mom and I had to forgive her and myself. I was finally able to spend time with my siblings. Me and my sister started hanging out, she told me she wished she could find a husband like I had, she asked me what happened between me and my husband, I couldn't bad talk my mother so I just told her I did wrong and ended my marriage.

My brothers played basketball, football, and many instruments in school. I made sure I was present for everything they had going on so they would know I loved them and enough time had been lost between us due to me not really coming around while I was married. My mom and husband just made me feel like I was wrong for moving forward in my life so I gave up what belong to me to make them happy. Not long after my divorce, my sister came to live with me. She had two sons. One born in the year of 2003 and the other in the year of 2004. Not too long after that, our mom became very ill, had to be hospitalized.

CHAPTER SIX

Things wasn't looking good for her at all. She was hospitalized for ten days released, two weeks later hospitalized again for another nine days. Had to learn to walk again, her speech and eyesight was affected also. During the times of the hospitalization, I made the decision for my brothers to stay at my home so we can all be together. I made sure my brothers, my nephews, and my kids got to school every day, got home from school and did their homework. I tried to make their life as easy as possible. I took all the grandkids to visit my mom while she was in the hospital, trying to get my brothers to go was like pulling teeth. I didn't understand why they didn't want to go see mom in the hospital. They finally went after asking several times. They were in charge of keeping their nieces and nephews while me and my sister helped with mom in the hospital.

I brought a CD player along with a gospel CD. We all stood around her bedside and sung I Need You to Survive. I spent countless hours at the hospital, still worked and kept the kids on the right track. When my mom was released from the hospital, Keith gave my sister and me his work schedule so my mom wouldn't be home alone. My sister and I would take turns sitting with my mom to make sure she made it to her appointments, had something to eat, and went to the bathroom. A couple times my mom was left by herself, with having to crawl to the bathroom to use it and crawl to the kitchen to get something to eat. I continued to pray and stay focused. Day after day, week after week, month after month, my mom's health got better. She was able to walk better, talk better and see better. My brothers went back home, my sister got her own place, so her and my nephews moved out; it was my girls and I all over again.

One day my brothers rode their bikes to my house, they said, "Shawny, mom told us what Keith did to you," I said, "she did?" I asked them why would she tell ya'll that. One said, "she told us he wasn't our biological father and that he had molested you when you were a child." I said, "yes he did, but I'm alright." They said, "we hate him for that." I said, "don't hate no one, hate is a very strong word, if I can still respect him and he did those things to me surely ya'll can." They both looked at me and said, "that was wrong to do those things to you."

CHAPTER SEVEN

I started dating and met someone. Had recently been released from prison after doing five years. He told me that was his past and wanted to live for the future. We started hanging out on the daily basis, always wanted to be around each other. After two months of dating I asked him, "is there something you want to tell me." He said, "yes, the woman I was with before dating you she is pregnant." I asked, "is she pregnant by you." He said, "yes." I asked him when did he find out, he said, "he knew for a while, she is five months." I started crying and asked him why he didn't tell me he said, he didn't know feelings would develop so fast, didn't want to take a chance on losing me. I told him if I would have known the day I met him I would not have went any further went with him. So now I'm crying, he's crying I'm questioning is there anything else, he saying, "please don't leave me, I want to be with you."

He grabbed his belongings (which weren't very much) from his grandmother's house and brought them to my house. He started driving my vehicle to later fall asleep behind the wheel and my car was towed. He had illegal items in his possessions. He was arrested. He had his mom call me on three way asking me to bond him out. He apologized, told me he wanted to be out to see the birth of his child, I felt sorry for him. I did bond him out. He was released, to only be taken back into custody three months later when he went to see his parole officer. The officer read the police report noticed the illegal items that were found in his possessions. He was in violation of his parole so he went to prison.

He called me while in prison and told me how he didn't have anyone else to be there for him, he asked me was I going to leave him; I asked him can I think about it, he said he want to know now. I had never been with a man that went to prison or spent time in prison. All I could think about if that was me I would want anyone to leave me, I told him I will be with him, I wouldn't leave his life. I had no idea he would use me mentally, physically, emotionally and financially.

I sent him money every week, sent several letters to him, on one occasion he received eleven letters from me, kept money on the house phone and cell phone so we could talk every day, I would drive 2 1/2 hours to visit him, some weekends I would rent a motel room to stay and visit for a weekend. After being in prison for ten months, he received a letter saying he had to answer for the charges for the illegal items that were found in his possessions when he had the accident in my car. His bond was set at $1700. Two months later, I paid the $1700 to have him released. He got out and he asked me to get him a lawyer. I signed the bond money over to the lawyer to take his case. We went to court and he took a plea deal, he received three years' probation. We were so happy he didn't have to go back to prison.

I thought he was happy because he had a good woman that loved him and was in his corner, but what I find out a short time later shocked me. I asked him why are you leaving every night and coming in 3am, 4am, and 5am. He said, "I be at my grandmother's house." I asked why? He said, "that's my home and going to always be my home."

He grabbed some of his belongings and said, "come drop me off at my grandmother's house."

He became physically abusive even striking me in my face giving me a black eye. I couldn't understand why he was treating me this way. When he went to prison, I stayed with him, paid the money to get him out, supported him through his case but yet he was quick to verbally and physically abuse me, he would grab a trash bag put his stuff in it and told me to take him to his grandmother's house. This one particular time I dropped him off, I came back to his grandmother's house four hours later and see a car parked in front of the house. I called his phone got no answer, I knocked on the door and rang the doorbell, got no answer. I sat outside and waited. Two hours went past, he walks out and a woman walks out. I walk up to her and said, "I'm Shawny." She looks at me and says, "I know who you are, he tells me everything, I'm his daughter's mom, I'm not going to quit messing with him, I love him." I asked her when he needed $1700 to get out of prison was she messing with him then, he told me to leave. He got in the car with her and pulled off, all I could do was look at the car go down the street. I didn't hear from him for seven days.

The seventh day he called me sounding sad, telling me how he missed me and how he was sorry for what had happened, he asked me to come pick him up from his grandmother's house. I didn't hesitate, I said, "I'm on my way" I ran out the house and went to pick him up. We just embraced each other and said we wouldn't talk about it. As time went on he continued to leave driving my vehicle every evening and coming in back 3am, 4am and 5am every morning always claiming he was at his grandmother's house sometimes calling me from his grandmother's phone so I would believe he was there. Until one day I went to his grandmother's house for Thanksgiving, one of the neighbors stopped me to chat, asking me how I was doing after seeing him pull off leaving me standing in front of his grandmother's home. The neighbor told me, "yes he's at his grandmother's house everyday but guess what? That same woman he pulled off with is the same woman he picks up and brings over here with him every night." I didn't know what to say. I paused and I said he calls me from time to time, the neighbor said yes I know I see him walking outside with the cordless phone while she is in the house. The neighbor said I'm telling you this because you need to move on with your life it's not fair for you to hold your life up for him. It was so hard to enjoy Thanksgiving after hearing that type of news. He is smiling in my face, telling me how he loves me, but can't wait to drop me off at home while so him and his daughter's mom could be together.

Finally, enough was enough, one day we were together, was pulled over by the police; he had a warrant issued for his arrest and was taken into custody at that time. He was being sent back to prison. I asked him what he wants me to do now he is going back to prison; he had the audacity to tell me, do everything you did for that year I went away. I said so what you are saying is you want me to send you money every week, come see you for weekends at a time, keep money on the phone(s) so you can contact me, and write you letters. He said yes. I said tell you what, that woman you was with when you were out, tell her to do those things, I'm done, and I hung up the phone, blocked his calls. I finally started picking up pieces in my life.

Chapter Eight

My daughters and I moved into our new place. We had been at our new place for about three weeks. My daughter's where outside playing with other kids from the neighborhood. One of the kids asked me to meet her grandmother. I said, "yes." She showed me where she lived. My daughters and I went to meet her grandmother. I knocked on the door; this lady answered the door and greeted me with a big smile. She said, "hi I'm Lynn." I said, "I'm Shawny, me and my daughters just moved into the neighborhood about three weeks ago. Your granddaughter asked me to come meet you, which was a very good idea because I'm a concerned parent and want to meet the parents or guardians of the kids my kids decides to play with." She said, "I don't blame you, I'm the same way." She immediately opened her door and said, "come in." I walked in, we went to sit down. The kids asked could they play outside, we both said, "yes, so we can talk."

I explained I had recently got out of an abusive relationship and ready to start a new life. With no hesitation, she tells me, "I'm so glad you made it out of that situation." While we were talking, she went to the stove and started cooking. She said, "excuse me, we can continue to talk I just need to make sure I finish my dinner; I have a big family here with me. I have my grandkids and my great grandkids that live here with me." I started thinking to myself, "so she don't have a perfect life either." We continued to talk. Her dinner was finished; she offered dinner to my daughters and me. We ate dinner at her house, with her, her grandkids and great grandkids. I don't know how she had enough food to go around but it was enough for everyone to eat and get full. I thanked her for lending me her ear, the positive advice, and the dinner. She said you are welcomed, anytime. We left and went home. On my way home, one of my daughters asked me, "So did you enjoy being at Ms. Lynn house?" I said, "yes, she was very nice, she invited us into her home, we talked like we have been friends for years, and she fixed dinner and invited us to eat." The next morning came, I went back to her house, knocked on the door again, she opened the door, I said, "I hope I'm not disturbing you, I enjoyed our conversation so much yesterday I came back again to talk some more." She said, "that's fine, come in." I stayed over at her house for hours. She fixed us breakfast, lunch and dinner. My daughters showed up again. After dinner, she says, "I wish I could stay and talk but I have to get to Bible Study." My daughters heard her say her and her family was going to Bible study. I asked 'Ms Lynn, "what kind of church is it?" She replied and said, "It's a Baptist church." My daughters asked me if they could go to Bible study with her. I said, "it's okay with me if she says its ok with Ms. Lynn."

They went to Ms. Lynn and asked would it be okay if we go to Bible study with you? She said sure. I asked, "do you have room for them?" She said very politely, "there's plenty of room for them, no problem at all." I trusted my girls going with her and her family. Her grandkids and great grandkids were so happy my girls were going they all started jumping up and down saying yes I'm glad ya'll can go. I told them I would see them when they get back and I left and went home. When they returned from Bible study, both of them rushed through the front door, came to sit next to me and told me how they enjoyed Bible study. They said the Pastor was awesome; we would like to go back. I was so happy to hear they enjoyed Bible study. I asked, "how did Ms. Lynn treat you." They both said, "she was very nice, she fed us again before dropping us off at home. We asked her if we can go back and she said yes. She said Bible study is on Wednesday, choir rehearsal is on Thursday, and Sunday morning service." Sunday came, my girls asked if its ok with Ms. Lynn can, we go to church with her, I said, "yes." They went to ask Ms. Lynn could they go to church with her, she said, "yes." Not one time did she turn them down. They went to Sunday service, I stayed home. After Sunday service, they came home just as excited as they were after Bible study. They came in my bedroom and said we enjoyed the Sunday service. I said, "that's good, I'm happy to hear that." One of my daughters says, "what do you do at home while we are at church? What is so important that you have to send us off to church and you not go with us? I sat there with this surprise look on my face, I finally answered after thinking how do I answer this question. I then said, "I will go one day." She said, "One day, ok" very sarcastically and they walked out my room. Wednesday came, they asked can we go to Bible study, I said, '"yes." I secretly called Ms Lynn and asked did she have room for one more, I told her I would like to join them this evening at Bible study. She paused for a minute and said we would love to have you. I could feel the excitement through the phone. She made me feel like I was making the right decision at that very moment. I told her I would be over. My daughters said, "we are ready, we going to Ms. Lynn's house." I said, "Ok, let's go." They looked at me smiling saying, "You going?" I said, "yes." They both grabbed me and hugged me saying, "we are so happy you are going!" I said, "me too." We went to Ms. Lynn's house, she and the kids were walking out to go to the vehicle we all get in and headed off to Bible study. We pulled up to the church, everyone gets out, and we all walked to the door and walk in. My daughters immediately walked in as if they were walking in the front of our home. They pulled me by the hand as if they were two years old, walking up to men and women saying, "this is my mother", I was shaking hands, hugging people, and shaking more hands and hugging more people. They were saying, "Hi mom, glad you can make it, we are members walking in but once you walk in and the door closes behind you, you become family."

I walked in feeling full of shame, thinking they could see me as that child that was once molested, physically abused by her mom's boyfriend whom she later married, a failed marriage, and an abusive relationship and my broken heart. I hid behind my beautiful smile. My daughters said, "come on, it's time to meet the pastor, he's in his office." We walked to his office the door was closed, they knocked on it saying, "Pastor, we have a surprise for you." He said, "come in." They rushed in before me saying, "our mom is here," very excitedly. I felt like a celebrity. The Pastor stood up embraced me and said, "welcome to Greatest Baptist Church, we are glad to have you come visit, we hope you will enjoy this Bible study and return." I said, "I hope so also, at this time I do not have a church home, my daughters came home and told me enjoyed Bible study and the Sunday service." I also told him, how my youngest daughter asked me what do I be doing at home that's so important that I can't go to church with them, she said they felt like I was pushing them off to church and not going with them. They always knew we stood together and fell together so why change. He said to me, "you have some beautiful daughters, GOD speaks through children also." I just smiled and said, "thank you." One of the members knocked on the door and said, Pastor, we are ready for Bible study." I left his office and went to sit down. The Pastor comes out of his office and sits in a chair in the front of the room while everyone is facing him, after he sits down I see my daughters, one sitting on his left side and the other one on his right. They saw me with this confused look on my face and says, "oh yeah, we are the Pastor's Bible study readers." I was lost for words. I said, "that is so good." They would read the scriptures from the Bible and the Pastor would explain it. I enjoyed Bible study so much, I said, "I can't wait to come to Sunday service." I experienced the teaching, now it was time to hear the preaching. Sunday finally came.

I attended what I thought would be Sunday service, turned out to be Sunday Worship. The Pastor started preaching, one of the things he said stuck with me, he said, "I don't look like what I been through." I couldn't wait to get home to look in the mirror. I had to look at myself not in the natural but the supernatural. I continued to attend Bible Study and Sunday Worship week after week. My oldest daughter went to Ms. Lynn and the Pastor and said she wanted to be baptized. I was so surprise to hear that news. I asked her was she sure, that's what she wanted to do. I knew that at age twelve, I was forced to be baptized. My daughter said this is one of the many things I would like to do. My daughters and I became members of Greatest Baptist Church and Easter Sunday, we were baptized. They became more involved with the church. Not only where they the Pastor's readers in Bible Study, they also started praise dancing, my oldest daughter begun singing in the choir. We continued to attend Bible study and Sunday worship.

CHAPTER NINE

It was a week before our one year anniversary of being Baptized, my oldest daughter came to me while I was sitting down watching TV. She says, "mom, we were told to keep something from you." I said, "who told you to keep something from me?" She said, "Granny." She went on to say that granny told her she would take care of it. I said, "if granny can tell you to keep something from me and you do it, maybe I don't need to know, so don't tell me." Then I asked her, "did granny take care of it?" She said, "it's been eight years and I'm still waiting on her to take care of it." I said ok let granny handle it. All I could think about is why my mom wouldn't want them to tell me, is it because she loved me so much she didn't want me to hurt or was it to cover up something she didn't want me to know.

The next day I talked to my friend, Shavonda, I told her my daughter came to me and told me my mom told her to keep a secret from me, and I told her if someone can tell you to keep a secret from me and you do it than maybe I don't need to know. Shavonda stood there with this very serious look on her face, with tears in her eyes and said to me" you are wrong for that, you need to talk to her and find out what it is, you are her mother and she is crying out for help. I said, "Shavonda," she said, "Shavonda nothing, don't do that, find out what it is, she didn't tell you then and now she wants to tell you." I went home soon as my daughter got home from school she came thru the door I said sit down; tell me, "what you were trying to tell me yesterday, what you were told to keep from me?" No mother could have prepared herself for what she was about to say.

She said, "your brothers use to make me and my sister put their penis in our mouth and in our vaginas." I said, "which brother?" She said, "both of them." One would take me in his room and the other would take my sister, sometime we would be in the same room. Most of the time it happened at granny's house, but when they came to our house while granny was in the hospital it would happen at our house also. She said, "they would yell at us, hit us and tell us to open our mouth then they would put their penis in my mouth, take my clothes off, tell me to lay down and open my legs, I didn't know what they was doing, all I know is when they got up I would be in pain down in my private area along with blood, sweat from their bodies would be on my body." I asked how many times did it happen? She said, "several times, every time we would go to granny's house." I then asked, "how old were you and your sister when this happen." She said, "my sister was four years old and I was seven, they stopped when I turned nine, your brothers were fourteen at the time." She also recalled one time one of the boys put their penis is her sister's mouth and she vomited. I asked, "what did they do after they finished?" She said, "they would laugh, our bodies would be wet and sticky." I asked, "how did granny find out?" She said, "your nephews would be there sometimes seeing them take us out the room with them, they would grab us and pull us away while we were trying to hold on to our cousins hand saying no we don't want to go." Our cousins would run to granny in her room and say, "the boys are doing nasty stuff to our cousins. She would pull out a belt and start whooping them, while she is whooping them she is saying that didn't happen, stop lying. When my sister and I tried to tell granny she also whoop us, and tell us we were lying. She would call everyone in the room and have us say what they did to us right in front of them, they would deny it, and soon as we leave her room, they would put their hands on us and curse at us. They continued to do those things to us." My oldest daughter said, "she got jealous when they got girlfriends." I was so lost for words. I said, "ok, I'm glad you told me."

My youngest daughter came home from school; I sat her down and asked her, she had this surprise look on her face like how do you know? She hesitated at first; I told her you don't ever have to worry about seeing them again. She cried and said, "yes mom, they made me and my sister put their penis and our mouth and they hurt me down there." After she told me, she said, "it felt like a ton a bricks was lifted off her chest." I went in my room, fell to my knees, I cried out, "Father GOD, In the Name of JESUS, I can't do nothing with this situation, I need you to handle this one, my heart is broke." I remember one of the stories in the Bible about Judas betraying JESUS with a kiss. I was betrayed not only by Renee (my mom) but by my brothers also. Eight years had went past and no one told me anything. I cried that whole night, tossed and turned, couldn't sleep.

The next day when my Heavenly Father woke me up, I was reminded, He won't put more on you than what you can bear. He prepared me for this when I was a child starting at age seven. I had to work on forgiving those who knew what was going on and didn't do anything to stop it even if it took to tell me to never bring my daughters around again; I also have to forgive the ones who did those horrible acts to my innocent daughters. I never thought this would happen to my daughters, my mom assured me they wouldn't be left alone with Keith, she assured me she wouldn't let what happen to me happen to them. My daughters were treated like a filthy rag. To this day, I do not speak to Renee or my brothers. This is a chapter in my life I will never forget. This has brought my daughters and I closer. I couldn't save my daughters from this horrible experience; I hope this book will inspire others. If anything is going on that hurts you, tell it, I don't care what anyone says. If you have experience, any type of abuse, sexual, physical or mental, don't be afraid to talk about it. Don't let the ton of bricks weigh you down. The bricks are the actions of what someone else has done to you.

Printed in the USA
CPSIA information can be obtained
at www.ICGtesting.com
JSHW010251020824
67246JS00010B/157

9 781365 827921